Prepare Now to Succeed on Your Mission

Prepare Now to Succeed on Your Mission

LOREN C. DUNN

BOOKCRAFT, INC.
Salt Lake City, Utah

Library of Congress Catalog Card Number: 76-50447
ISBN 0-88494-313-5

3rd Printing, 1978

Lithographed in the United States of America
PUBLISHERS PRESS
Salt Lake City, Utah

Dedicated

to my father
who wisely said of my own mission call
"You have two years in which to
serve it and the rest of your life to think about it"

and to my father-in-law
who was a missionary all his life

Ye Sons of God go forth
Sound a call to all the earth
As a witness to mankind
Help the lost their way to find
In this the dispensation
of fullness of times
The dispensation of fullness
of times

Ye Sons of Adam arise
Lift your voices to the skies
Ye defenders of the faith
Like the father of your race
In this the dispensation
of fullness of times
The dispensation of fullness
of times

Ye Sons of Israel prepare
Make each soul on earth aware
Send your cry into the world
Gospel's standard is unfurled
In this the dispensation
of fullness of times
The dispensation of fullness
of times

Christ has paid the price for all
By atonement, from the fall,
Now he says we must go forth
To each nation on the earth
And hail the dispensation
of fullness of times
The dispensation of fullness
of times

— Loren C. Dunn

Contents

Preface   ix

A Mission Call   1

The Four Questions   6

A Missionary's Expectations   20

Adjusting to a Mission   24

Adjusting to a Companion   27

Building and Sharing Your Testimony   32

Bearing Testimony of the Book of Mormon   39

Mission and District/Stake Organizations   44

An Elder Writes   48

Finishing Your Mission   57

Waiting for a Missionary   63

What Parents Can Do   66

Index   75

Preface

Almost every missionary comes into the field with certain expectations. These are based on such experiences as listening to returned missionaries, watching missionaries in action, making personal missionary preparations, and the influence of family and friends.

So unique is missionary service that it is difficult for the expectation level of the missionary to be the same as the actual experience. This becomes significant when one realizes that a person's ability to succeed in a new situation is linked to the way he has expected that situation to be.

A missionary will have a better opportunity to succeed if he can balance the experiences of missionary preparation and anticipation with what is actually expected of him in the field. The closer his expectation level is to the actual mission experience, the more successful he will be and the easier the adjustment.

It is also important for the missionary to keep his expectation level flexible. When it is set too firmly, any deviation between expectation and actual experience creates difficulty.

One successful mission president put it in this way: "Often the more successful missionaries are those who have already experienced a number of disappointments in athletics, at work, at school, or elsewhere. I have discovered during my two mission experiences that those missionaries who have most successfully dealt with disappointment in the past deal more effectively with the mission field than do others with a more limited background. Maturity seems to encourage realistic expectations. These missionaries often do well because they roll with the punches and take good and bad experiences as they come. Most new missionaries, unfortunately, go through somewhat painful adjustment periods when they are bringing their expectations into reality. This is absolutely necessary in order that they might adapt to the challenges of missionary work successfully."

The aim of this book is to help prospective missionaries get a feeling for missionary life and what will be expected of them in the field. It also offers some suggestions to those at home who are seeking to help. It does not deal with the established priesthood programs of the Church for missionary preparation or missionary service; it would be presumptuous to do so.

If it can in some way assist the prospective missionary in establishing a level of expectation closer to the power and vitality of actual missionary life, then it will have accomplished its goal.

Chapter 1

A Mission Call

"We believe that a man must be called of God, by prophecy, and by the laying on of hands, by those who are in authority to preach the Gospel and administer the ordinances thereof." (Article of Faith 5.)

There is no better demonstration of this belief than when the Lord calls a member of his church to a full-time mission. How is the missionary call extended, and how is the mission assignment determined? To help you understand what to expect, here in brief are some of the procedures.

Before a call is extended, the prospective missionary must be recommended by local priesthood leaders. The earliest this can happen is generally at age nineteen for a young man and age twenty-one for a young woman. There may be, however, some variation in certain areas of the world.

The bishop (or branch president) calls in the prospective missionary for an interview. This normally would be a continuation of the interviews he has had with the person over the years. It is a searching interview to determine the individual's desire for missionary service, moral worthiness, and any other matters that might have a bearing on whether he or she should be recommended for missionary work.

If the bishop feels that everything is in order, he fills out a missionary recommendation form, which is then signed by the prospective missionary. On the back of the form the bishop gives his confidential appraisal of the missionary candidate.

The prospective missionary also receives a missionary medical form, part of which he fills out, while the remainder is completed by his family physician after a physical examination. Good physical and emotional health is an important prerequisite to a successful mission.

The doctor sends the medical form to the bishop, who evaluates it and then sends it along with the missionary recommendation form to the stake (mission district) president. After reviewing the information on the forms, the stake president invites the prospective missionary to a private interview. If all is well, he adds his confidential recommendation and sends all of the information to the Church Missionary Department.

The missionary recommendation form is reviewed for completeness by the Missionary Department and is then placed with other recommendations for assignment to a specific mission area. The assignments are made under the direction of the Council of the Twelve, with assistance from other General Authorities, each being given careful and prayerful consideration. There are instances too numerous to mention which clearly demonstrate that each prospective missionary is called of God by inspiration to a specific mission location.

The suggested assignments are then sent to the President of the Church, who makes the final determination. The President then sends the letter of call to the missionary.

This sacred letter calls the missionary to his particular mission and tells him when to report to the Missionary Home in Salt Lake City or to the Language Training Mission (LTM) in Provo, Utah. Missionaries who live outside the United States or Canada may be asked to report directly to their missions because of the time and expense involved in traveling to Salt Lake City. Usually a missionary is asked to report to the Missionary Home or the LTM six weeks to two months from the time he receives his call. This allows time for all necessary preparations.

Enclosed with the call is an acceptance form on which, in his own words, the missionary accepts his call. This form is to be countersigned by the bishop and returned to the Missionary Department.

Other materials are also sent to help the missionary in his preparation. If he is being called to another country, for example, he will receive information on what immunization shots to have and how to obtain a passport. A personal letter from the mission president will give him such information as what clothes to bring.

A few days before he enters the Missionary Home, the prospective missionary and his family meet with the stake president, who, acting under the authority of the President of the Church, will set the missionary apart to serve in the mission to which he has been called and will give him a blessing pertaining to that service. To ensure that all is in order the stake president will have a confidential interview with the missionary just prior to his being set apart and again immediately before he leaves for the Missionary Home.

Only those missionaries who are going to English-speaking missions report to the Missionary Home in Salt Lake City. There they participate in a five-day training session during which time they are instructed in becoming disciples of Christ, in learning the discussions, and in the "how-to's" of missionary work. They go directly to their fields of labor from the Missionary Home.

If a missionary lives outside the United States or Canada, he reports directly to his mission. Instructions on how to report will come with his letter of call. Under the direction of the mission president, he will go through an orientation which will cover the same basic material that is offered at the Missionary Home in Salt Lake City.

If he lives in the United States or Canada and is called to a non-English-speaking mission, he will report directly to the Church's Language Training Mission in Provo, Utah. He will be there for approximately eight weeks. Four objectives have been established for the missionaries at the LTM: (1) to become disciples of Christ, (2) to learn the mores and culture of those among whom they will labor, (3) to learn the language and also the missionary discussions in that language, and (4) to learn the "how-to's" of missionary work.

The calling of a missionary in The Church of Jesus Christ of Latter-day Saints is carefully designed to allow for the inspiration of the Lord and to provide help and assistance necessary so that each missionary can succeed in his calling. Each one, then, is "called of God, by prophecy, and by the laying on of hands, by those who are in authority...."

As the Lord indicated in a similar context, "... Whether by mine own voice or by the voice of my servants, it is the same." (D&C 1:38.)

Chapter 2

The Four Questions

Each prospective missionary needs to answer at least four questions before he accepts a mission call:

1. Am I capable of doing the work?

2. Is my life in order so I can answer a call worthily?

3. How will I be supported financially?

4. Do I really have a desire to go?

Capability

Judging from the comments of many missionaries, one of the common concerns at the very beginning of their missions is fear — fear that is born of an inward doubt about their ability to do missionary work.

It is not uncommon for a missionary to wake up one morning in the Missionary Home or early on his mission and say, "What on earth am I doing out here?" This is part of the normal adjustment for most missionaries — normal, that is, unless the missionary thinks he is the only one who feels this way and therefore is having special problems. So unique is a mission experience that one can't quite know what it is like until he has experienced it.

The newly called missionary wants to do what is required of him, but he isn't quite sure what to expect. He has seen the pages and pages of missionary discussions to be memorized, not to mention the scriptures associated with each discussion. Many have seen other missionaries in the field — their disciplined and dedicated way of life, the way they meet people and speak in church, the way they go out and knock on doors. It is not unusual for a prospective missionary to have doubts. What he does not realize, however, is that every missionary in the field was at one time very much like him: asking the same questions and wondering the same things.

A number of years ago I wanted to learn how to type, so I took a typing class in school. I remember the first day, sitting in front of that typewriter and looking at all those keys. I was convinced that I could not learn to type. I would never have told anyone this, but that is how I felt.

Then the instructor came into the room. He had been teaching this class for many years. "I guarantee that if you finish this course you will know how to type," he said. "In fact, in all my years of teaching I have never failed to teach a student to type if he finished the course."

He then began, in an orderly way, to take us step by step through the process of learning how to type. He taught us the positions of the fingers and how each finger was responsible for certain letters. After each step was explained we would practice it until we could do it with some skill; then we moved on to the next step. We were given individual instruction manuals so that, after the instructor got us started, we could move ahead at our own pace. The instructor was there to help us with special problems and to give us tests. And in spite of how I had felt in the beginning, I learned how to type.

This experience can be likened to being called on a mission. First and foremost, the Lord has called you, and he never calls a person to a position but what he opens up a way for that person to fulfill the calling. "And if it so be that the children of men keep the commandments of God he doth nourish them, and strengthen them, and provide means whereby they can accomplish the thing which he has commanded them. . . ." (1 Nephi 17:3.) This does not mean that it will be easy, but it does mean that if you are constantly prayerful and follow the established procedures each day with a willingness to learn, a spirit will gradually come into your life in a way that will change you and make you equal to your calling. The change will be gradual but unmistakable. This is called "getting the spirit of your mission," and it is special because of the special nature of your calling and your determination to serve the Lord.

Second, you will be taught how to learn and memorize in an orderly, step-by-step fashion in the Missionary Home, Language Training Mission, or mission field. Some will learn more quickly than others, but all who prayerfully follow the guidelines with determination will learn.

Third, a resolution from the beginning to see the mission through to the end will help the missionary who finds that one phase or another of missionary work is offering a special challenge. Some may become impatient when things don't fall into place immediately. To realize that you have two years in which to fulfill the calling will help you do your best each day and not try to do it all at once.

"Therefore, my beloved brethren, be ye stedfast, unmoveable, always abounding in the work of the Lord, forasmuch as ye know that your labour is not in vain in the Lord." (1 Corinthians 15:58.)

Some mention needs to be made here of the person who may have a physical, a mental or an emotional handicap that would prevent missionary service. The President of the Church has said that those who are not able to go are not required to go. These would include those who are confined to wheelchairs or who have other physical impediments that would hamper them in the service that is required of a full-time missionary. It would also include those who have a handicap in either reading or writing, since the nature of missionary work demands these skills. The same is true for those who have severe health or emotional problems. Such problems are almost never cleared up in the mission field. In fact, the pressures of missionary work usually make them worse.

A person who finds himself in these circumstances should not construe this to mean that the Lord does not want his service. A review of one's patriarchal blessing, for instance, will show that the Lord expects certain things of each of his children, and he blesses them with those talents and abilities needed to accomplish these special expectations. If it is not full-time missionary work, perhaps it is stake missionary work. If not that, then most assuredly it is some other avenue of service in the Lord's kingdom.

"For all have not every gift given unto them; for there are many gifts, and to every man is given a gift by the Spirit of God. To some is given one, and to some is given another, that all may be profited thereby." (D&C 46:11-12.)

Worthiness

To be worthy is to keep the commandments of God.

Some years ago there was a sign over the door of the football dressing room at Brigham Young University: "If you do something wrong once, it's a mistake. If you do something wrong twice, it's a habit."

We spend our lives developing either good or bad habits. Some think that addictive habits apply only to smoking, alcohol, and drugs. While it is true that the use of such substances can lead to addiction, there are many other kinds of addiction that need to be avoided. Immorality can become addictive. So can profanity. So can bad personal habits.

The Lord has said, "Ye shall know the truth, and the truth shall make you free." (John 8:32.) No one is so free as the person who has decided never to engage in a wrong act. He doesn't have to worry about what it might do to himself or others. He doesn't have to worry about how it might affect his relationship with the Lord. He doesn't have to worry about whether he will do it again. He is truly free — free to go before the Lord without embarrassment; free to participate in the Church and its programs without embarrassment; free to associate without embarrassment with those whom he respects most; free to be comfortable in his own company; free to be called by the Lord to any position in the Church.

Years ago the Boston Red Sox had one of the greatest relief pitchers in professional baseball. If the team could just carry a lead into the middle or late innings, this pitcher would come in and secure a victory. It was a relief to the fans to see him come in from the bullpen when the team had a lead. They knew he would save the game.

Some have the mistaken feeling that life is like that. "I'll do anything I want to do now. In a few years I'll stop and begin living the life I should live. I'll suddenly move into the mature adult world and do the things I should do."

There is no magic time when a person suddenly becomes an adult, no magic moment when the responsibilities of adulthood are suddenly placed on one's shoulders. No one will suddenly call us out of the bullpen and onto the mound. The truth is that everything we have done and are doing right now is conditioning us for what we will be for the rest of our lives. Elder Richard L. Evans once said, "You had better be satisfied with the road you are on, because it will take you where it is going." Someone else said,

"The sins we do two by two must be paid for one by one."

If a person is morally clean, if he is worthy to go on a mission, he is in the best possible position. All the good alternatives of life are open to him. If there are those who have made serious mistakes, remember that the atoning blood of Jesus Christ was shed for them as well as for the rest of us, and they can be forgiven if they repent. "For behold, I, God, have suffered these things for all, that they might not suffer if they would repent." (D&C 19:16.)

One thing is certain: changing one's life, repenting, right now, no matter how hard it seems, is easier than doing so next week or next month. If it's going to happen sometime, then why not now?

It was on Lexington Green in Massachusetts that the first battle of the American Revolution took place. Advancing were the well-equipped and well-trained British soldiers. Lined up across the green were the Minute Men with their leader, Captain John Parker. The Minute Men were not professional soldiers. They had no uniforms. Only one thing united them: the determination to secure their own freedom and the freedom of their families. As the British moved forward, Captain Parker uttered these famous words: "Stand your ground. Don't fire unless fired upon, but if they mean to have a war, let it begin here." The Minute Men did stand their ground, and that was the beginning of a new nation.

There is usually a time in everyone's life when he has to take a stand and make a beginning.

If necessary, take a stand and let repentance begin now. This may require a confidential chat with your father and/or your bishop. Only the Lord can forgive you, but the bishop can clear you for future activity in the Church. He can tell you if you are on course. Get your problem cleared up and then determine with your bishop the possibility of missionary service.

"Believe in God; believe that he is, and that he created all things, both in heaven and in earth; believe that he has all wisdom, and all power, both in heaven and in earth; believe that man doth not comprehend all the things which the Lord can comprehend.

"And again, believe that ye must repent of your sins and forsake them, and humble yourselves before God; and ask in sincerity of heart that he would forgive you; and now, if you believe all these things see that ye do them." (Mosiah 4:9-10.)

Occasionally, because of fear or other reasons, a missionary tries to get into the mission field without clearing up previous transgressions. A few are even under the mistaken impression that if they delay their confession until they are in the mission field they will not be sent home. Nothing is more pathetic than the person who attempts to deceive the Lord. The missionary who does this comes into a work where everyone depends on the Lord's Spirit day by day; yet he does not qualify for that help. He finds himself out of step. He struggles to do the things missionaries normally do. He puts himself through a kind of hell. Finally he comes to the mission president, anxious to know what he has to do in order to get the load off his back. How can he square himself with the Lord?

The Church then has to make some decisions, all of which are embarrassing to the missionary. First, the missionary has to write letters to his stake president and bishop to clear up any unfinished matters and apologize for not telling the whole truth. It may also be deemed necessary for such a letter to go to the father of the missionary.

Next, the mission president gets a recommendation from the missionary's bishop and stake president as to what they feel the course of action should be. The mission president adds his own recommendation and sends it to the Missionary Executive Committee, which makes the final decision. It is not uncommon for a missionary to be sent home at his own expense, or to be sent to Church headquarters in Salt Lake City for a special interview, or to be placed on probation for the rest of his mission. All of this, plus some painful memories in years to come, could have been avoided if the prospective missionary had been completely honest in his confidential interviews with his bishop and stake president prior to leaving on his mission.

If the missionary commits serious moral infractions while in the mission field, this usually means Church court action.

Finances

The question of who will support you financially on your mission must be answered and arrangements made well in advance to take care of this necessary part of your mission.

The responsibility of financial support follows the same order as the priesthood welfare responsibility. First, the individual is expected to work and save for his own mission. Second, if more assistance is needed, it becomes the responsibility of the missionary's family. Third, if still more help is needed, the local priesthood quorums and the ward or branch are asked to assist.

For those outside the United States and Canada there is assistance available from the Church Missionary Fund, but not until a wholehearted effort has been made by the other sources mentioned in the previous paragraph.

We have discovered that there is a relationship between the success of a missionary and how much he sacrifices in his own behalf. The Church recommends that a mission savings account be started for each young man at a very early age. This will help him to keep his mind on that goal and encourage him to save his money for that purpose.

Most missionaries are financed with a combination of funds from their own savings and funds from their parents. The statement that "sacrifice brings forth the blessings of heaven" was never more true than in missionary service.

Every family that supports or helps support a missionary can testify from personal experience that the Lord pours out his blessings upon missionary families. Here two missionaries tell of their experiences:

1. "My parents make their living on a small farm in the south, and they have had a struggle to keep me here. Last summer a hailstorm destroyed the crops on every farm around us, but our place was untouched. On our side of the fence the corn stood green and tall; on the other side, it was beaten into the ground. The Lord knew we had to have that crop to keep me in the mission field."

2. "My sister recently went on a mission, and my father knew he would have trouble in financially supporting both of us. He went to his bishop and asked for a blessing to enable him to do so. The bishop said: 'That won't be necessary. We can ask the elders quorum to keep one of them out until the other comes home, and then you can take care of it all right.' My father said, 'That isn't what I want. I want to support them myself. You just give me a blessing so I can.' The bishop gave him a blessing. The next Monday when he went to work there was a check on his desk for $1,000 with a note from his employer saying 'We appreciate your services and dedication. Please accept this token of our appreciation.' "

Perhaps this will not happen in every case, but it does show that the Lord suits a blessing to those who financially support his great missionary work in the world.

The only question left is, Can it really be called a sacrifice if it calls forth the Lord's blessings? King Benjamin says:

"And now, in the first place, he hath created you, and granted unto you your lives, for which ye are indebted unto him.

"And secondly, he doth require that ye should do as he hath commanded you; for which if ye do, he doth immediately bless you; and therefore he hath paid you. And ye are still indebted unto him, and are, and will be, forever and ever; therefore, of what have ye to boast?" (Mosiah 2:23-24.)

Desire

"Therefore, if ye have desires to serve God ye are called to the work." (D&C 4:3.)

Most young people in the Church basically want to do the right thing. They sometimes get sidetracked, however, because the world has different standards than they do, and after a while this worldly or materialistic approach to life becomes all-important.

Not long ago a successful businessman came to see me. He told a very interesting story as to why he did not go on a mission. When he was young his family was very poor. They had to go without many things in life and had to work hard for what they did have. He related that he was quite old before he tasted fresh milk; canned milk mixed with water was less expensive. He told of wearing a girl's coat one winter because it was given to him and it was all his parents had to keep him warm. As he grew into his teens he became interested in cars; in fact, his greatest desire was to own a new car of a particular make. He got a job and carefully saved his money until he had enough for a down payment. It was a great day when he brought that car home, because he had sacrificed a long time for it.

About that time he and his friend were asked to see the bishop one night after sacrament meeting. His friend went in first, and the bishop said, "We would like to recommend you for a mission." His friend was half expecting this, and after discussing it for a few minutes he told the bishop he would accept a call.

Then the young man who had just bought the new car entered the bishop's office. The bishop extended to him the same invitation to prepare for a mission, but the young man said: "Bishop, I can't go on a mission. I'm paying for my car."

As a result, he never did go, and here he was now, relating his story. He told of how in the intervening years he had felt uneasy about his decision. He said it reached the point where he felt embarrassed when he went to elders quorum meeting because most of the elders were returned missionaries and he was convinced that they knew more about the gospel than he did. They were probably not better versed than he was, but that is how he felt. He said that to this day he cannot look at a car of the particular make and model he had bought without getting an uneasy feeling within himself, because the car represented a decision contrary to what the Lord had wanted him to do.

In everyone's life there is a similar temptation. Whenever the Lord, through his servants, seeks to call us on a mission or to any responsibility in the Church, there is always that car or motorbike or job or some other worldly object to try to get us to turn away from or to delay the Lord's call. But the momentary pleasure of owning that new car, motorbike, or whatever, never lasts. One is then left with the memory of the decision he will have to live with forever. "Choose you this day whom ye will serve; . . . as for me and my house, we will serve the Lord." (Joshua 24:15.)

Chapter 3

A Missionary's Expectations

I received a phone call from a missionary who had been in the mission field only a few weeks. The voice on the other end of the line was anxious and deeply concerned. The missionary needed to talk to someone; and not having been out long enough to know he should have contacted his mission president, he called me.

The problem was one of adjustment — not uncommon, especially in the early weeks of a mission. The elder didn't realize this, however, and he was convinced that there must be something wrong with him because he did not feel right about doing the Lord's work. He had kept the matter to himself, trying to work it out. This was commendable, but when the problem did not resolve itself he made a mistake by not going immediately to his mission president, the person endowed by the Lord with the inspiration and skill to give immediate help.

I chatted with the elder for a few minutes and answered some of his questions. I also assured him that what he was going through was part of the adjustment process which every missionary experiences to a greater or lesser degree. This seemed to help him somewhat. Then I referred him to his mission president for the real help.

For missionaries, the challenge of adjustment and overcoming obstacles is a common one. This may not be generally realized, because returned missionaries don't usually talk about this part of their mission. Almost every Latter-day Saint has listened to a missionary report his mission in sacrament meeting. Usually he tells about the highlights of his work; he focuses on the mountain peaks. He does not always rehearse the day-to-day work that conditioned him, the ways in which the Lord brought him through the valley and up the slopes so that he would be capable of such achievements.

The missionary says, "They were the best two years of my life" — and so they were. But they were years of adjustment, of overcoming weakness, of meeting trials head on, and, in the process, of being smoothed and molded into an effective servant of the Lord. "I am like a huge, rough stone," said the Prophet Joseph Smith, "rolling down from a high mountain; and the only polishing I get is when some corner gets rubbed off by coming in contact with something else. . . ." (*Teachings of the Prophet Joseph Smith*, p. 304.)

The men who climb Mount Everest have to scale a number of lesser mountains in order to arrive at their base camp. This helps to condition them for the big climb. Once the mountain is conquered, the climber seldom tells about what it took to get to the base camp. A description of the actual climb is more interesting and inspiring than a review of the preparation and conditioning. So it is with missionary work. A missionary focuses on the great spiritual experiences of his mission, and some may think a mission is filled with nothing but spiritual experiences. They see the course of a missionary as this: ——————. Actually, missionary work is closer to: ∿∿∿.

The Lord has wisely made it this way so that the missionary can grow. When a missionary is motivated and filled with the Spirit, when he is on one of the peaks in his mission, it is easy to do the work. When he is in one of the valleys, he has to work harder and pray harder. It is in the valley that growth occurs, where a missionary gets closer to the Lord, where faith is developed, where character emerges. When the missionary understands what is happening to him and stays with it, such experiences in the valley of trial lift him to ever-increasing heights.

When one is filled with the Spirit and all is going well, it is easy to do missionary work. These special times come as a gift from the Lord. When the missionary is in the valley of effort and trial and still maintains his performance, that is his offering to the Lord, and it will be answered with a blessing. "For after much tribulation come the blessings. Wherefore the day cometh that ye shall be crowned with much glory; the hour is not yet, but is nigh at hand." (D&C 58:4.)

Through this kind of experience the missionary develops the quality of consistent performance. A consistently good performer is always in demand, whether in the Lord's work or in life generally.

Chapter 4

Adjusting to a Mission

Some diplomats who have to travel long distances are forbidden by their governments to enter into serious negotiations immediately upon arrival at the destination. This is because "jet lag" may cause them to make unwise decisions. Doctors explain it in this way: We all have a sort of alarm clock in us. Through the daily habits we establish, the body expects us to eat at certain times and to sleep at certain times. When we travel to a far-off place where the time might be a number of hours behind or ahead of what we are accustomed to, our alarm clock is thrown off. Until the body gets accustomed to the new schedule, it still expects to do things the old way. For the first few days a person may be dozing off at four in the afternoon and waking at three in the morning.

Missionary work is the same way. For nineteen, twenty, or twenty-one years a person conditions himself by everything he does. These are usually years of growing and developing, of acquiring likes and dislikes, of cultivating friendships, of learning to live and get along in a world that knows very little or cares little about spiritual things. Some have not yet had to assume any great responsibilities. Others have developed their own ways of doing things.

One of the great evidences of the divine nature of the Church's missionary work is to see thousands of these young men and women come together. Each brings his own personal background and set of experiences with him, and each has the opportunity to become a dedicated, responsible servant of the Lord. A divine call and a determination to serve the Lord have changed many a "fun-loving kid" into a mature, responsible missionary whose parents hardly recognize him upon his return home.

Between the time a missionary is called and the time he gets the spirit of his calling is the period of adjustment — when the missionary's worldly clock gradually slows down and his spiritual clock starts up. Missionary work is a totally different way of life, and every missionary should anticipate the adjustment. An elder can hurry the adjustment process by committing himself wholeheartedly and looking ahead, not back.

An airline stewardess who was a good member of the Church was once asked if her job did not make it hard to live her religion. Her answer was no. She said: "All you have to do is decide in advance what kind of a person you're going to be. Then you don't find yourself getting into any difficult situations because your decisions have been made in advance."

This is good advice for the missionary. He needs to decide in advance what kind of a missionary he is going to be. When he reaches the mission field his thoughts should no longer be dominated by parents or girl friends or things back home. This may take some time, but it can be done. He will be living a daily schedule that will direct him toward the spirit of his mission, but it requires a willing heart. The apostle Paul said: " . . . with fear and trembling, in singleness of your heart, as unto Christ; . . . as the servants of Christ, doing the will of God from the heart." (Ephesians 6:5-6.)

Those who love the missionary can help him with this adjustment. (This help is discussed in a later chapter.)

Chapter 5

Adjusting to a Companion

"And ye shall go forth in the power of my Spirit, preaching my gospel, two by two, in my name, lifting up your voices as with the sound of a trump, declaring my word like unto angels of God." (D&C 42:6.)

One of the great experiences in missionary work is the opportunity to pursue one's calling with the help and encouragement of a companion. But it requires patience, cooperation, and willingness to accept the differences between oneself and other people in order to make a companionship work.

A missionary companionship is unique. At home, a young person chooses his friends on the basis of mutual likes and dislikes. Friendships develop with people one can get along with. Even then, best friends see each other only when they want to, and they don't spend every waking moment together.

In a missionary companionship, the Lord chooses one's companion. The divine selection seems to be based on what qualities need developing. The missionary is with his companion twenty-four hours a day. They pray together. They work together. They study together. They enjoy success and failure together. They see each other at their best and at their worst. The strong points and weaknesses of both become apparent. But through it all they are together.

One of the greatest blessings of a full-time mission comes from these companionships. Forging a working relationship as servants of the Lord also teaches one how to get along with people no matter what differences there may be in personality or background.

In this kind of sacred companionship, missionaries can help each other in the spirit of unity and cooperation. Rather than condemn each other for weaknesses and bad habits, such companions can gradually help each other to improve as, in the spirit of love and meekness, each helps the other to overcome objectionable traits.

Three traits seem necessary for a companionship to work well. One is the ability to overlook things that might seem to be objectionable in one's companion but do not necessarily affect the worthiness of the companion or the success of the work. The Lord promises that if we develop the ability to forgive others their trespasses, he, in turn, will forgive us in like manner. (See D&C 82:1.) On this basis, members in general and missionaries in particular should want to constantly forgive one another so that they might themselves be eligible for the forgiveness of a loving and just God.

Another necessary trait is illustrated in the missionary labors of Ammon in the Book of Mormon. When King Lamoni befriended Ammon and offered his daughter to Ammon in marriage, Ammon, the great missionary, made this statement: "Nay, but I will be thy servant." Thus Ammon became a servant to King Lamoni. (Alma 17:25.) The secret of missionary work is to approach the people as their servant. A servant of the Lord is a servant of the people. When a missionary can see himself as a true servant of the Lord, not only to the people among whom he is laboring but also to his companion, his effectiveness is greatly increased.

One missionary said: "When I become upset with my companion, I shine his shoes or do something else for him that I don't have to do. This seems to help us both. It not only improves our feelings toward each other, but there is an increase in the Spirit of the Lord." King Benjamin in the Book of Mormon expressed it in this way: "And behold, I tell you these things that ye may learn wisdom; that ye may learn that when ye are in the service of your fellow beings ye are only in the service of your God." (Mosiah 2:17.)

There is no more powerful instrument in the hands of the Lord than two companions who are in harmony with their calling and acting as one. They have the Spirit of the Lord with them. Their teaching is smooth and effective.

A final element necessary for a companionship to be effective is the ability to work. At a mission-home testimonial the night before he was to return home, a successful missionary reflected back and said simply,

"The more you work, the less discouraged you get." That same evening another soon-to-be-released missionary said: "I'm very thankful that it has been hard — two of the hardest years of my life. But I needed it to refine me and test me."

Hard work and living the missionary rules leave little time to think about individual differences, the girl back home, or other things that get in the way of adjustment.

A new missionary arriving in the field has the security of knowing that following the orientation at mission headquarters he will be assigned to an experienced senior companion. The new missionary will learn from the senior companion the day-to-day procedures of missionary work. A good senior companion will be a hard worker because he will have the responsibility of helping his new companion over the initial adjustment that all missionaries face.

The mission leaders hold the senior companion responsible for the companionship. He is expected to help his companion learn how to teach the gospel. He is also expected to teach his companion correct mission procedures and to make him thoroughly acquainted with the missionary handbook. He is expected to do these things in love and friendship and according to the discipline established by the mission.

A good senior companion, in partnership with the Lord, will in turn prepare a junior companion to receive a new missionary. A good senior companion will train a junior companion to be even better than the senior. In this way the mission, the work, and the missionaries will be constantly improving.

Being a junior companion is an ideal opportunity to receive training in priesthood organization. The Lord has organized the Church so that each person can have the benefit of direct divine inspiration and also the help of a presiding officer. A person who knows how to look to his presiding officer unlocks for himself an additional source of help and inspiration in the Church. The Savior was the perfect example; he made it clear that he only did that which the Father sent him to do. He was completely obedient to his Father. Nephi the prophet said: "Know ye not that he was holy? But notwithstanding he being holy, he showeth unto the children of men that, according to the flesh he humbleth himself before the Father, and witnesseth unto the Father that he would be obedient unto him in keeping his commandments." (2 Nephi 31:7.)

The Lord blesses those who can demonstrate their ability to follow priesthood leaders. He has said: "He that is ordained of God and sent forth, the same is appointed to be the greatest, notwithstanding he is the least and the servant of all." (D&C 50:26.)

Being an energetic junior companion who is willing to accept and follow the advice and guidelines of a senior companion and other mission leaders is an essential beginning to missionary service.

Chapter 6

Building and Sharing Your Testimony

"Behold, verily I say unto you, for this cause I have sent you — that you might be obedient, and that your hearts might be prepared to bear testimony of the things which are to come." (D&C 58:6.)

Testimony is revelation from God that Jesus Christ is his Son, that Joseph Smith was a true prophet of God, that the President of The Church of Jesus Christ of Latter-day Saints is the Lord's prophet on the earth today, and that the Church is the kingdom of God on the earth.

This knowledge cannot come from men. It cannot come through earthly knowledge. Testimony comes through prayer and faith and a sincere desire. It is a witness of the Spirit, sent from our Heavenly Father, which touches one's soul in such a way that he knows divine truth. It is more of a spiritual experience than an emotional one. When one is touched by this Spirit, he *knows* the Church is true. His whole soul comes alive with this realization.

Earthly knowledge can be challenged. Perhaps something is true that we have read or studied or been told. Perhaps it is not. But a testimony is an ultimate experience. It comes from God. It is truth in its purest form, and when an individual is touched by that Spirit, he knows.

A testimony is fragile. It depends on one's ability to cultivate the Spirit of the Lord. When worldliness causes a person to offend the Spirit, his testimony suffers.

Connected with an active testimony are definite spiritual experiences — perhaps the answer to prayer, the healing of the sick, or the promptings of the Spirit to do or not to do certain things. But if a testimony is not nourished, these spiritual experiences will grow more distant and in time may even be rationalized by the worldly mind as being something less than they actually are. At this point the person is struggling, because he has usually ceased doing the things which will bring him a distinct spiritual confirmation of that which is true. The prophet Alma wrote: "But if ye neglect the tree, and take no thought for its nourishment, behold it will not get any root; and when the heat of the sun cometh and scorcheth it, because it hath no root it withers away, and ye pluck it up and cast it out." (Alma 32:38.)

No discussion of testimony is complete without some comment on faith. One definition of faith is complete trust and confidence in the being, purposes, and words of God. Faith precedes everything in the Lord's work. "And I work not among the children of men save it be according to their faith." (2 Nephi

27:23.) If a person has enough faith to experiment on the words of the Lord, he will gradually come to know that the work is true. He will have the beginning of his own testimony.

"But behold, if ye will awake and arouse your faculties, even to an experiment upon my words, and exercise a particle of faith, yea, even if ye can no more than desire to believe, let this desire work in you, even until ye believe in a manner that ye can give place for a portion of my words." (Alma 32:27.)

The depth of a person's testimony can always be determined by what he does. Unlike belief, testimony requires commitment and definite action. It leads to right action no matter what the conditions, no matter what the social consequences. One person has said, "Having a testimony means one will live the commandments of the Lord even if he is all by himself on a desert island." Having a testimony means establishing one's own relationship with the Lord, a living Savior who knows his children by name. What a person does each day is influenced first and foremost by that relationship.

With that background, let us look at the challenges some new missionaries face regarding testimony.

I sat in a Sunday School class as a teacher told the following story about himself. He said that he had been reared in a community close to Salt Lake City, and he attended to his Church duties according to how convenient they were for him. After he married, his job took him to a small community away from Utah. The branch was small and needed the active participation of everyone. Soon he was involved in teaching a class and performing other duties. He found this to be one of the great challenges of his life, and it was here that the gospel really began to mean something to him. Upon analyzing the situation, he came to realize that this was the first time he had really committed himself. Up until this time he had been giving lip service to his religion but had never really had to commit himself.

For some, the same is true when they enter missionary service. For one reason or another they have never had to fully commit themselves prior to their mission. Now suddenly they are meeting scores of people each day and telling them the Church is true. They are living an entirely different kind of life. There are spiritual and physical and social adjustments.

It is not unusual for a new missionary in this kind of setting to say: "Wait a minute. Many of these people seem good people. Is the way I am teaching the only way to return to the presence of God?"

The missionary may also have doubts arise in his heart when he finds that that which he has said is true now requires a day-to-day commitment of faith, prayer, and hard work.

For some missionaries these questions usually arise in the first part of their mission, and, as a result, they find themselves doubting their own testimony. They say to themselves, "Should I be out here telling other people the Church is true when I am not sure myself?"

Honest doubts are healthy for a missionary if they are handled right. The truth is able to stand up under the strongest scrutiny. If a missionary will use his doubts to sincerely seek and pray in search of the answers, he will be rewarded with greater testimony and a closer relationship with the Lord. "If any man will do his will, he shall know of the doctrine, whether it be of God, or whether I speak of myself." (John 7:17.)

If the missionary uses his doubts as an excuse not to commit himself and to stop working and to do nothing, he paralyzes himself with his own questions. Under the direction of their mission president, most missionaries have used their doubts to move forward in greater commitment and to gain an abiding testimony. A few have used their doubts as an excuse to do nothing.

As a young man, Heber J. Grant was called by the Brethren to go to Tooele, Utah, to become president of the Tooele Stake. A number of priesthood holders living in Tooele must have questioned that move. Imagine bringing in someone from the outside to preside over one of the established stakes of Zion! Furthermore, on the Sunday he was sustained, Heber J. Grant got up and said he thought the Church was true — not that he *knew*, but that he *thought* it was true.

After the meeting some of the local people crowded around President John Taylor, who had come to Tooele to present President Grant's name to the stake. They must have said something like this: "First you bring someone from outside to be our stake president, and now he says he is not even sure the Church is true."

President Taylor is reported to have smiled and said, "Brother Grant knows the Church is true, all right; he just doesn't know that he knows."

At the following stake conference, Heber J. Grant bore a powerful and vibrant testimony. Years later he became the seventh President of the Church.

So it is with some missionaries. A mission helps them to know that they know. Any missionary can convert his doubts and questions into strong testimony and go on to serve a successful mission.

In the mission field, a missionary who is seeking from the Lord a confirmation of his testimony can usually receive it in at least four ways:

1. Whenever a missionary says he has doubts about his testimony, it should be determined whether he is committed to the missionary rules, including the handbook, and is faithfully following them. Those who wholeheartedly commit themselves to do this find that they establish a pattern of prayer, study, and work, which in turn puts them in a position for the Lord to bless them with what they need for the building of their testimony.

The missionary handbook contains guidelines that have been accumulated from the total missionary experience of the Church. The handbook, if followed, will help a missionary get into the spirit of his mission in the shortest possible time, and will help him stay in that situation; always provided that he follows the handbook's principles from the beginning of his mission to the end.

2. Another item that builds testimony in new missionaries is the discussions themselves. A returned missionary put it well when he said: "Before my mission I had gone through the programs of the Church and had been taught the gospel. But it wasn't until I learned the discussions that I saw the principles of the gospel together in an orderly sequence. It strengthened me to see how well everything fitted together." New missionaries grow in faith and testimony when they go through the gospel discussions in the same manner in which an investigator is asked to study them. This is especially true when it comes to reading the Book of Mormon, a matter which will be discussed in another chapter.

3. A third testimony-builder in a new missionary is the observing of the literal change in the lives of his investigators as they start to accept the gospel. The change that the Spirit works in an individual who is undergoing the conversion process is unmistakable. It is an inspiration to all who see it, and in itself it helps build testimony.

4. Testimony comes when one learns he can and must rely on the Lord. If the missionary is doing his part in the day-to-day activities of missionary work, the Lord will literally guide him and bless him.

Chapter 7

Bearing Testimony of the Book of Mormon

As a missionary you will bear testimony of the truthfulness of the Book of Mormon to those among whom you labor. This testimony can come to you as you study the Book of Mormon, ponder its teachings in your heart, then put to the test the promise given by Moroni: "And when ye shall receive these things, I would exhort you that ye would ask God, the Eternal Father, in the name of Christ, if these things are not true; and if ye shall ask with a sincere heart, with real intent, having faith in Christ, he will manifest the truth of it unto you, by the power of the Holy Ghost." (Moroni 10:4.)

The Book of Mormon is a compilation of the writings of prophets of God who were part of the great civilization that lived anciently in the Americas. These prophets taught the gospel of Jesus Christ as did their counterparts in the eastern hemisphere. They prophesied of the birth and life of the Savior, also of his death and resurrection — even though these events were to transpire in another part of the world.

The highlight of this great record is the appearance of the resurrected Savior to these people. He taught them the same gospel and principles of salvation that he had presented to those who were his disciples in the Holy Land. It was only a matter of three generations from that time, however, before the people had almost entirely rejected the teachings of Jesus Christ. They had become warlike and even sought to murder the prophets.

One of the last prophets to live was a man named Mormon, who took all of the records and abridged them into one book. For this reason the volume is known as the Book of Mormon. Mormon passed the sacred records to his son Moroni, who was one of the last followers of Christ in that generation, and who was himself hunted because of his beliefs. It was made known to Moroni and to other prophets that the Lord would bring this record forward in a later generation of time to testify of the events that took place in Jerusalem and to convince mankind that Jesus Christ is the Son of God and that there is a plan whereby man can be saved and receive eternal life.

Being commanded of the Lord, the prophet Moroni buried the record in a hill, where it remained until the year 1827, when a young man by the name of Joseph Smith was shown by a divine messenger where the record was hidden. Through power given him of God he translated it so that the world might have a second evidence that the basic truths of the Bible are correct.

There were witnesses to the translation of these plates. In a joint statement, Oliver Cowdery, David Whitmer, and Martin Harris gave the following testimony: "BE IT KNOWN unto all nations, kindreds, tongues, and people, unto whom this work shall come: That we, through the grace of God the Father, and our Lord Jesus Christ, have seen the plates which contain this record. . . . And we also know that they have been translated by the gift and power of God, for his voice hath declared it unto us; wherefore we know of a surety that the work is true."

The reason for the Book of Mormon coming forth in this generation of time can be found on the title page of the book, which is part of the translated record and which says, in part, "And also to the convincing of the Jew and Gentile that JESUS is the CHRIST, the ETERNAL GOD, manifesting himself unto all nations." The Book of Mormon, then, is a means whereby men can be convinced that God lives and that Jesus Christ is his Son and the Redeemer and Savior of the world.

The Book of Mormon bears record of the divine sonship of Jesus Christ and recognizes him as Redeemer of the world. These passages from Third Nephi are a good example: "Behold, I am Jesus Christ the Son of God. I created the heavens and the earth, and all things that in them are." (3 Nephi 9:15.) "Behold, I have come unto the world to bring redemption unto the world, to save the world from sin. Therefore, who so repenteth and cometh unto me as a little child, him will I receive, for of such is the kingdom of God. Behold, for such I have laid down my life, and have taken it up again; therefore repent, and come unto me ye ends of the earth, and be saved." (3 Nephi 9:21-22.)

A second message of the Book of Mormon is to teach mankind the plan of salvation in its pure and basic form so that we might know what the Lord expects of us if we are to be saved. Again, an example of this can be found in the words of the Savior in Third Nephi: "And this is my doctrine, and it is the doctrine which the Father hath given unto me . . . and I bear record that the Father commandeth all men, everywhere, to repent and believe in me. And whoso believeth in me, and is baptized, the same shall be saved; and they are they who shall inherit the kingdom of God." (3 Nephi 11:32-33.) At the same time, the Savior commissioned certain disciples with specific authority to perform this baptism. He also explained what is meant by repentance.

Finally, if the Book of Mormon is true, then it must attest to the fact that Joseph Smith, the translator of this record, was a prophet of God and was divinely inspired to bring forth this work. In a revelation concerning the coming forth of the Book of Mormon the Lord referred to Joseph Smith in the following way: "He has translated the book, even that part which I have commanded him, and as your Lord and your God liveth it is true." (D&C 17:6.)

Joseph Smith once made the statement that the Book of Mormon was the keystone of our religion, and that a person could get closer to God by following its precepts than by any other book. Joseph Smith has long since passed away; but The Church of Jesus Christ of Latter-day Saints and the Book of Mormon live on as a sign and witness to all nations that Jesus Christ is the Son of God, that there is a way to return to the presence of God, and that the basic truths of the Holy Bible are correct.

Today the Church is known as The Church of Jesus Christ of Latter-day Saints to distinguish it from the Church of Christ that existed at the time of the New Testament and the Book of Mormon. As in the ancient church, it has apostles and prophets at the head, and it teaches that all mankind can be saved through obedience to the principles and ordinances of the gospel of Jesus Christ. We believe that the Savior literally leads his church through direct and continuous revelation to its leaders. We believe too that all mankind are the sons and daughters of God, and that if they will prayerfully and honestly seek him he will bless them with a realization of the truthfulness of these things. We believe that Jesus Christ will come again to the earth, and when he does he will reign as King of kings, as the resurrected Lord, as the Prince of Peace.

The Book of Mormon, then, is the bridge between an unbelieving world and the gospel of Jesus Christ. Speaking of Joseph Smith and the coming forth of the book, the Savior said: "And gave him power from on high, by the means which were before prepared, to translate the Book of Mormon; which contains a record of a fallen people, and the fulness of the gospel of Jesus Christ to the Gentiles and to the Jews also . . . proving to the world that the holy scriptures are true, and that God does inspire men and call them to his holy work in this age and generation, as well as in generations of old." (D&C 20:8-9, 11.)

Chapter 8

Mission and District/Stake Organizations

Missionaries need to understand how missions, districts, and stakes are organized in order to work more effectively with members in accomplishing missionary work. Here is the basic organization of each of these units as they pertain to missionary work.

Mission Organization

A mission is presided over by a mission president who has been called by the Lord. He and his family live in the mission field, usually from two to three years.

Assisting him are two counselors called from the membership of the mission, who help the president with ecclesiastical responsibilities pertaining to members of the Church.

The mission president also calls two assistants from among the full-time missionaries to help him with supervision of the missionaries and the proselyting program.

Zone leaders are called from among the full-time missionaries to supervise from twenty to fifty missionaries in the various zones of the mission. There are two zone leaders in each zone, and they are companions.

The zones are divided into districts. The mission president calls from among the full-time missionaries a district leader in each district to supervise from two to five sets of missionaries. The district leader has a missionary companion.

Each missionary in the field has a companion. At first a missionary serves as a junior companion, but as he learns and gains experience he may be called to be a senior companion.

The mission president may also call four full-time missionaries to be his office staff. They work in the office during the day and proselyte in the evenings. Those who work in the office usually are called to that responsibility for no more than six months, after which they go out into the field again.

Every six weeks to two months the mission president has a private interview with each missionary. He also conducts a zone motivational and development meeting for all missionaries in a zone every six weeks to two months. Each week every missionary is expected to send a report and write a short letter to the mission president.

The district leaders, zone leaders, and assistants to the president are constantly working with their fellow missionaries in addition to proselyting in their own areas. In each district, regular meetings are held for motivation and training.

While this overall organization might vary slightly from mission to mission, it is the basic mission structure.

Member District and Stake Organization

Each mission is organized into districts, with the organization similar to that of a stake. Within each district are branches, which are similar to wards. A district is under the direction of the mission until it becomes a stake; it then works independent of the mission, although extremely close cooperation is maintained regarding missionary work.

In each ward or branch, a ward or branch mission leader is called from among the members. In a stake he is a seventy. He meets once a week with the other priesthood leaders in a priesthood executive committee meeting. As part of this meeting he reports on all missionary work in the ward or branch and enlists the help of the other priesthood leaders. His report includes such matters as: who is being taught by stake and full-time missionaries in the ward; what special projects, such as open houses, are being planned; the progress of missionary-oriented programs; and the friendshipping of nonmember families by member families.

The full-time missionaries meet with the ward or branch mission leader each week in a correlation meeting to share referrals and coordinate missionary work. The important thing for full-time missionaries to remember is that they should always go through the ward or branch mission leader when dealing with members.

Chapter 9

An Elder
Writes

With the writer's approval, I have included below
some excerpts from a series of letters from a missionary which were written at regular intervals during
his two-year mission. They illustrate how a missionary develops a testimony of the Book of Mormon and
the gospel of Jesus Christ, and they give much in-
sight into the personal growth which missionaries
experience as they devote themselves to the work of
the Lord.

Second Month Out

"I have been in the mission field seven weeks now
and have finished memorizing the Uniform System
for Teaching Families. While I was memorizing these
discussions, I did what will be the most important
thing for me — ever. I converted myself to the gospel.
I *know* that I am here serving the Lord, not just
because of some other reason. My testimony has
grown more than I ever thought possible in the past

few weeks, and it is strengthened each time I see what the Lord is doing here in this mission. I know that with his help, anything can be done."

Fourth Month Out

"I can testify to you that the Lord is blessing me here on my mission. I have been transferred to a new area, and we have been blessed with many people to whom we can teach the message of the restoration. Last night we committed a family (consisting of a father, mother, and three children under three years of age) to be baptized on the 14th of June.... My testimony has grown over the past four months from the tiny thing that it was into the testimony I now have which is a testimony of the truthfulness of the gospel, that Jesus is our Savior, and that God does live. I have had the spiritual witness that the Book of Mormon is true and is the word of God to us as well as to the descendants of Nephi and also the Lamanites."

Sixth Month Out

"I have been very blessed in the past few weeks, especially in being able to find a golden family to work with. The family is really seeking the truth and reading and studying the Book of Mormon. Still, they will be baptized only with the help of the Lord. I have been called to train a new elder, and in the last few weeks that we have been together, I have learned more than I thought possible. I am understanding more and more what missionary work is all about.... Now we are teaching five families, all with children of baptismal age, and the five families are searching for the truth."

Eighth Month Out

"The Lord's work is really the greatest work any person can be engaged in.... He gives more pay, help, and everything else than any employer on this earth. All we have to do is to ask, and he gives freely what we need.... He has blessed me especially in my position of training a new elder, and I know that without His help we wouldn't have been able to bring those whom we have brought into the gospel.... I am looking forward to this coming Sunday when I will be able to listen to the general priesthood meeting [from Salt Lake City].... The ward ... is now really finding success with the member-missionary program, and people are being brought into the gospel as a result of it. They are beginning to realize their responsibility as members who have been 'warned.' "

Tenth Month Out

"First, I would like to wish you a merry Christmas and a joyous New Year. The past months have been filled with much work and success. A few weeks ago we tracted out a woman and left her a copy of the Book of Mormon. When we called back the next week to pick up the money for the book, she told us that she had read it and wanted to be baptized into the Church. From there it went great. She wrote her husband in _____ and he has investigated the Church there. A week ago she told us that he had set the baptismal date for the entire family after Christmas. It is great to see the effect the gospel has in the lives of people who accept it. I've really gained strength to my testimony because of the different experiences I've had in teaching people and watching them react as their testimonies grow. . . . I've come to learn that the Lord does help those who ask for his help, and I've learned to ask for help in all things."

Fourteenth Month Out

"These past two months have really been a bit of a challenge to me and my companion, but we have been blessed with success in our labors and are looking forward to the time when we will be baptizing a young boy and his mother. They were interested in the Church as a result of his coming along to an Aaronic Priesthood-Young Women's meeting. In this small branch of the Church the members are extremely close, and it is great when we take an investigator to church and see the members come up and introduce themselves and make the investigator feel like a long-time member. . . .

"I know that the gospel is true, and one reason in particular is because my mother, through the power of the priesthood, has recovered from a hip deterioration that would have put her in a wheelchair in the next few years. My dad wrote to me and said that for the first time in many years she was able to dance with him. He said that she even *ran* up a flight of stairs the other day. A few months before I entered the mission field she couldn't walk one hundred yards without sitting down to rest. . . .

"I've received more blessings in the last year than anytime before in my life. A month ago my sister was married. Her husband was baptized four days before the ceremony. They will be going to the temple as soon as possible, and I will be able to go with them and see them be united for eternity. The gospel is true. I've nearly finished reading the Book of Mormon for the fourth time, and I've fallen in love with it."

Sixteenth Month Out

"Everything that happens to me has helped me to grow and progress in one way or another. I can look back over the past year and few months and see the effects that I have had on others in bringing them to an understanding of the gospel message. The time is disappearing. I seem to have misplaced a year because it doesn't seem that I have been here this long. . . .

"I am in a small town about seventy miles north of _____ . There is a small branch of the Church here, and the membership is great. Just two nights ago we missionaries held a special fireside with the members to get them enthused about the priesthood correlated friendshipping program and their responsibilities. It was a success, because we got the support that we needed, particularly from the new branch presidency. Just a few weeks ago the stake president came up for branch conference and challenged the members to work on bringing their friends and neighbors into the gospel. The promise was made that if the membership grew to three hundred by next year, it would be made a ward. That has given the members incentive, and now things look good here. . . .

"Just a few weeks ago we were able to baptize a young lady who has been waiting for the gospel for two years. She had originally heard about the Church from one of her friends at work, and after she read the Book of Mormon and got a testimony of it, her parents stepped in and stopped her from being baptized. She had to wait for two years until she turned twenty-one and was old enough by law to join without her parents' consent. Now, after she has become very active in the Church, she has influenced her parents, an aunt, and other friends, and soon we hope to be able to teach her whole family the gospel. . . .

"I know that the gospel is true — there is no shadow of a doubt left. Whenever I get a question now, it is answered when I pick up the scriptures or the *Ensign*. It seems as if the Lord is just pouring out information upon my head, and all I have to do is be in a receiving attitude. This is what I have to work on."

Eighteenth Month Out

"May I begin by first saying that there have been many things happen to me on my mission. And now that I have only six months left, I can look back at what has already been the greatest time of my life. The best thing is that I can look back with satisfaction on my work. . . . I have changed greatly, and it would take me many hours to explain all of the many changes that this mission has made in my life, because every day I change and every day I notice some area in my life that has improved. . . .

"The Lord has blessed my companion and me with the opportunity of teaching and baptizing the greatest man I have been permitted to teach thus far on my mission. . . . We met Brother _____ at a friend's home. . . . We spoke with him about the Book of Mormon and then placed a copy with him and asked, 'If you knew that the Savior's church had been restored to the earth, would you like to know more about it?' It was four weeks from that time until he was baptized into the Church. . . . During that time Satan tried many times to dissuade him and also us. When we first taught him, both my companion and I were so ill that we could hardly walk up the hill to his house. During the discussion we each received much assistance from the Holy Ghost, and it was then that we challenged him to be baptized and he accepted. We met with him at least once a day from that time until after he was baptized. It was two weeks before we both regained our health. . . . Now, after Brother _____ has been in the Church for one month, we begin to realize just why Satan was trying so hard. . . . Brother _____ is sharing the gospel with everyone he comes in contact with, and every chance he gets, he is working at the chapel. . . . He is a leader and a strong member of the Church. . . .

"I am also beginning to see how much the Book of Mormon means to me, and I am setting life-long goals that deal with it. I am sorry to say I had never read it until I got out here on a mission, and I have read it five times since then. I wish I had spent some of my earlier years in reading the Book of Mormon, because I know it would have helped me over many a rough situation during that time of my life. The main help that it would have given me is strength to my testimony of the truthfulness of the gospel, and that would have helped me make up my mind earlier in life as to what principles I would have. When I get with new companions, . . . the first thing I make sure they do . . . is read the Book of Mormon. Then they don't have to rely so heavily on others' testimonies . . . but rather they . . . have one themselves."

Twentieth Month Out

"My companion and I were privileged to prepare (or *help* prepare) a young man for baptism. He is a person who was similar to myself a few years ago, so I felt very close to him and learned to admire him for the decisions he made. He was just at the point in life where a lot of serious questions needed to be answered, and it made a great change in his mixed-up life. He was able to recognize the truth when we presented it to him, and he had the courage to want to accept it. . . .

"I know the gospel is true, and I am sorry to see this brief two years rapidly drawing to a close. I look forward to being able to see many more people come into the gospel before the end of my mission and then helping friends back home find the Church."

Twenty-second Month Out

"Everything is well with me, except the after effects of a cold seem to linger on longer than they should. We have been working extremely hard in the past few months with little or nothing to show from it. We are placing more copies of the Book of Mormon than usual, but everyone wants to wait until after Christmas before they will take the time to hear the message of the restoration in their homes. I know that the Lord is saving up blessings for us at some future time, but I sometimes wish that they would come *now*. I guess I'm starting to become like the children of Israel under Moses . . . so used to blessings (and miracles) that when they don't appear, I get impatient. But I realize that the Lord knows best. . . .

"Today I have been in the mission field for twenty-two months, so you know that my time is growing short. It keeps slipping past faster and faster, and too soon I won't have any time left. . . . This is the last letter I'm going to send to you from here. . . . I hope to deliver the next one in person."

Chapter 10

Finishing Your Mission

"And now, behold, whosoever is of my church, and endureth of my church to the end, him will I establish upon my rock, and the gates of hell shall not prevail against them." (D&C 10:69.)

We have previously discussed the divine nature of a missionary call. Now let's look at the importance of fulfilling that calling.

Unlike the decision to attend a university or change jobs, a mission call comes from the Lord, and therefore it is more than a personal matter. This can be demonstrated by the experiences of a few who, at their own insistence, did not finish their missions. In each instance the encouragement of local priesthood leaders, family, and even General Authorities was to no avail. Yet with this decision comes the lingering feeling in one's heart of unfinished business, the tendency over the years to try to explain when no one is asking questions.

A young man came in to see me one day and said he wanted to go back to finish the mission he had left a few years ago. His wife had just had a baby, and there had been complications with the child. A priesthood administration was performed, and the child was healed. This brought to the surface feelings this young father had harbored in his heart for many years.

"When I realized what the Lord had done for me when I had not completed my service for him, I knew I had to go back," he said. "Brother Dunn, we have it all worked out. When my wife gets out of the hospital, she will take the children and move in with her family. I will sell the house, and I'll have enough money to finish my mission." There is something about a call from the Lord to serve a mission that stays in the heart.

I talked with this earnest young father for some time. I explained that his mission in life was now to take care of his family, to raise sons in preparation for missionary service. When the children are raised and there are fewer demands on the time of this young man and his wife, they could then be called as a missionary couple. He asked for a blessing, which I was most happy to give him.

The next example involved a young man who had had severe adjustment problems for some weeks before he finally left his mission. Upon his return home he went back to school in an effort to try to find himself. As it turned out, he roomed with a young man who was also a member of the Church and who had decided to make himself worthy for a mission call.

One day the roommate who was anticipating a mission call came to see me. "How does your roommate feel about your going on a mission?" I asked.

"He told me that it was my business, and if I wanted to go, I should go," he replied. Then he added: "But he also said, 'No matter how hard it gets, never come home early, because if you do, you will always be sorry. No matter how hard it gets, never come home early.' "

A third example involves a young missionary from the United States who was called to serve a mission in Great Britain. He had a disease that affected his back. He had had the disease before he left on his mission, but he had learned to live with it. The damp climate of Great Britain aggravated the condition, however. He was checked by a doctor there who confirmed his problem and recommended that he be released. He received an honorable release for medical reasons.

A few months later the young man came to see me. "I want to go back and finish my mission," he said. I checked his record and learned of his history. I told him not to be concerned; he had received an honorable medical release, and certainly the Church could not require any more of him as a full-time missionary. His response was short and touching: "Yes, but in spite of the pain, I think I could have made it."

A final experience took place in the mission field. A

few years ago while on a mission tour in Europe, I was asked to interview a young man who had recently arrived in the mission field and now wanted to return home. He had not been away from home before, and he was homesick and in despair in a strange country. He had actually run away once but had come back.

I had quite a long conversation with this missionary. From my own missionary experience I know something of the despair that can come into the life of a missionary when he first goes into the field and begins to make the initial adjustment. If he can just hang on through those early trials, gradually he will get into the spirit of his mission and find the peace and joy every missionary has a right to experience.

At first this missionary was adamant in his desire to return home, but gradually the spirit of the conversation began to change. We talked about his call from a prophet. We talked about his love for his parents and their desire for him to stay and succeed. We talked about those among whom he had been called to teach. Finally I asked, "Elder, do your father and mother want you home?"

He replied, "No."

"Do your brothers and sisters want you home?"

"No."

"Does your girl friend really want you home?"

"I guess not."

"Elder, does anyone want you home right now?"

"I guess not."

Then he said, with new determination, "Brother Dunn, I think maybe I had better try to stay." He had made a vitally important decision in his life — he had decided to hang on.

The months passed, and one day my secretary asked if I could take a minute to see a recently returned missionary. As I walked out of my office to greet the visitor, there was this same missionary. I didn't recognize him at first — he seemed taller because he was standing so straight. Unlike the first time we met, he looked me right in the eye, and his whole countenance was smiling. I can't remember what he talked about, but I shall never forget his image. He was going home now, a servant of the Lord, having completed an honorable mission. His roots were reaching downward, and although there would be the usual trials ahead, he knew something of what it means to hang on for a while longer when everything looks blackest.

From these experiences and from conversations with other missionaries we learn the following:

1. In the long run it is much easier to finish a mission than to come home early. Robert Louis Stevenson has said: "You cannot run away from a weakness. You must sometime fight it out or perish, and if that be so, why not now and where you stand?"

2. The divine nature of a mission call lifts it above almost every other experience in life. Whether the missionary finishes or not, it tends to stay with him.

3. Honest preparation is essential to successful missionary service. Make sure any problems of

worthiness are taken care of before the mission. Also, be frank and honest about physical and emotional problems on the mission preparation medical form. These problems are usually aggravated by mission service, and many times they may lead to early release.

4. In life, everyone has to learn to live with some aches and pains. The prospective missionary must not let these put him in the position of someday reflecting back and saying, "In spite of the pain, I think I could have made it."

Chapter 11

Waiting for a Missionary

Is it advisable for a missionary to have a girl friend waiting at home for him?

This question is a difficult one to answer. The decision as to whether a young woman waits for a missionary is a personal matter and must be determined by the persons involved. In making that decision, however, some of the following factors might be considered.

First, although I am not aware of a formal poll on the subject, it seems that more often than not an agreement to wait somehow gets sidetracked during the mission. As a result the missionary receives the familiar "Dear John" letter.

Any two people, especially those in their early adulthood, change over a period of two years. The special nature of missionary service, of course, causes the missionary to change, but the young woman changes also. Sometimes these changes are rather dramatic on both sides, creating a situation where a young couple almost need to become reacquainted following missionary service.

In light of this, several questions might well be asked:

1. Will waiting be good for the girl at home during the time when dating and social activity should be an important part of a young woman's life?

2. Will waiting be good for the missionary? Does having a girl friend at home cause him to become preoccupied with thoughts of her? In order to be successful, a missionary must serve the Lord with all his "heart, might, mind and strength" and "with an eye single to the glory of God." (D&C 4:2, 5.) Does the young woman who is waiting encourage that kind of loyalty and devotion?

3. Will waiting be good for the missionary work? If a missionary suffers, the work suffers. Certainly every Church member wants to do all within his power to help missionary work succeed, and the way missionary work succeeds is for the missionary to succeed.

If a relationship is mature and well-founded enough to take into account the above points, then it is likely that waiting for a missionary might be good, both for the work and for everyone concerned. Such a relationship would limit communication to a weekly letter and an occasional package from home. The tone of each letter should be uplifting and encouraging. The letters should ask the missionary about his work, tell about activities at home that are spiritual and positive, and avoid "wish you were here" themes. They should tell him how happy the girl friend is to have a missionary in the mission field. The encouragement of such a girl friend can help a missionary over hard times.

Some missionaries have told me that receiving recorded tapes from home can create problems. To actually hear the voice of a girl friend may develop in the missionary feelings of homesickness and cause him to become diverted from his work. For the same reason it is recommended that family and friends not telephone the missionary in the field except in dire emergencies.

Romantic involvements are strictly prohibited between missionaries and others within the boundaries of their mission. Not only do such involvements detract from missionary work, but they can also have serious consequences, such as Church court action and/or being sent home with less than an honorable release.

In addition, such feelings are impractical. While on a mission a missionary is living a different type of life. Spiritually and emotionally, he is on a different plane. One who feels he might be attracted to a young woman while serving in the mission field had best keep this in mind. His likes and dislikes when he is on a mission will usually not be the same as when he is at home. Thus, he needs to wait until he has been released and has returned home to determine whether the feelings he might have had for someone in the mission field are the same feelings he has in his everyday life.

Chapter 12

What Parents Can Do

"And as I partook of the fruit thereof it filled my soul with exceeding great joy; wherefore, I began to be desirous that my family should partake of it also; for I knew that it was desirable above all other fruit." (1 Nephi 8:12.)

One of the best preparations for missionary service has always been a mother and a father who live the principles of the gospel in their home. Most young people will have as much love and respect for the gospel as they see exhibited in the private lives of their parents. It is easier for a missionary to teach and testify about prayer, tithing, the Word of Wisdom, the Sabbath day, and other principles when he comes from a home where these are practiced. The Lord has admonished parents: "And they shall also teach their children to pray, and to walk uprightly before the Lord." (D&C 68:28.)

The emphasis of the missionary program of the Church is on the teaching and conversion of families.

The missionary discussions are designed so that missionaries can effectively teach family units. One of the principal ways of introducing the gospel to a family is for the missionaries to present a family home evening, to show how a home evening is held, and to actually involve the nonmember family. As the investigator family joins together in this activity, the missionaries take the next step and start teaching the whole family the discussions. This increases the number of family conversions, which brings added strength to wards and branches. A whole family joining the Church means they can help each other in their baptismal commitment. It is a better way than when only one or two in a family join and have to plan their Church involvement separate from the rest of the family.

A missionary who comes into the mission field having had the benefit of regular family home evenings has a decided advantage. He can teach this principle with confidence. He can bear testimony to its importance from firsthand experience. He can draw on his own background to demonstrate this program. He is well ahead of the missionary who has to pick all of this up after he gets into the field. One of the advantages of family home evening in every Latter-day Saint home is that parents are preparing their sons and daughters for future missionary service by showing them how it is done.

One of the great legacies a missionary can bring into the mission field is a home life that has clearly defined the role of father: A father who has established his position in the home by setting a good example and showing love and respect for the mother and the children. A father who provides leadership in the family and who does not leave the major decisions for mother to work out by herself. A father who has established himself as the spiritual leader in his home by holding family prayer, by seeing that family home evening is held with the whole family involved, by giving blessings to family members at appropriate times, and by demonstrating to his family a love and devotion to the Lord's work as he attends his meetings and fulfills his callings.

Mother plays a key role here because no father can fully accomplish the role the Lord expects of him in his home unless the mother is willing to support him in that role. It is the mother who teaches the children to follow their father and the priesthood. It is the mother who upholds the father in his role and gives him the confidence to succeed with his family.

Young people who learn to look to the role of father with respect and appreciation find this to be a help as they work in the Church. It is easier to respect and follow the bishop or branch president when there is respect for the priesthood leader in the home. It is easier for a family member to pray to a Heavenly Father when he understands and respects the role of an earthly father. And when a young man receives a mission call, it is less difficult for him to follow his mission president and the priesthood leaders appointed by the mission president if he has had a good relationship with his own father.

There are important lessons that a prospective missionary can learn within the walls of his home. Some of these are:

1. *Good personal habits*. The missionary day begins at 6:30 A.M. and ends at 10:30 P.M. A young man who has learned to get up early in the morning and go to bed at a decent hour at night will have an advantage. So will the missionary who has been taught good hygiene, such as daily bathing, brushing his teeth regularly, washing hands before meals, and so on. Ahead too will be the missionary whose mother has taught him the importance of eating regular, well-balanced meals and shown him how to prepare simple but nutritious foods.

2. *Work*. A young person who has been taught the dignity of hard work and who has been given responsibility at home will have an easier time meeting the demanding schedule of the mission field.

3. *Discipline*. A prospective missionary who has known discipline in the home will find it easier to follow the carefully planned days in the mission field and to get along with a variety of companions. "And when we obtain any blessing from God, it is by obedience to that law upon which it is predicated." (D&C 130:21.)

4. *Manners*. A young person who knows when to say "thank you," "excuse me," and "please," and who knows how to talk and eat with good manners will gain the trust and confidence of both members and nonmembers in the mission field. Members need to trust him enough to invite him to teach their nonmember friends, and good manners will help.

5. *Scriptures*. The tools of missionary work are the scriptures. No prospective missionary should go into the field without an acquaintance with the scrip-

tures, especially the Book of Mormon. The Church recommends daily scripture reading. This also offers many opportunities for mother and father to bear testimony to their family. "Seek not to declare my word, but first seek to obtain my word, and then shall your tongue be loosed; then, if you desire, you shall have my Spirit and my word, yea, the power of God unto the convincing of men." (D&C 11:21.)

6. *Personal care.* The first impression given by a missionary is most important. It can make the difference as to whether someone will listen to the message.

Every missionary should come into the mission field knowing how to wash underwear, socks and handkerchiefs, and how to press a shirt or suit. He should know how to sew on buttons and mend socks. Prospective missionaries may also need to learn such basics as shaving properly, shining shoes, tieing a tie, and hair grooming.

7. *Leadership.* Some missionaries erroneously equate success with holding the position of zone leader, district leader, or assistant to the president. They don't realize that the Lord rewards faithful missionary service with a greater outpouring of his Spirit and not necessarily with a leadership position. In the Church a person is "called of God by prophecy," and not because he covets a position. If parents could teach the prospective missionary to do his very best at whatever he is called to do, and not to "work" to be an assistant or a zone leader, the missionary will find real success and happiness in the mission field. He will also come to appreciate what it means to be called of God rather than to aspire to leadership.

While He Is Away

Here are a few do's or don'ts for parents that might help in their relationship with the missionary in the field.

Do write encouraging letters once a week. Avoid themes that will make him homesick. Ask about his work, and write about spiritual and uplifting experiences at home. Tell him how thankful you are to have him in the field.

Do write to the mission president directly if you are not hearing from your missionary on a regular basis or if his letters hint of serious health or other problems. (You may wish to talk with your bishop or stake president before making this inquiry.) The mission president interviews him about every two months and receives a weekly report and letter from the missionary. In addition, a district leader works with the missionary once a week, and the zone leader also sees him on a regular basis and reports to the mission president. Each missionary is well supervised.

Don't phone the missionary in the field except under the most extreme emergency conditions. Similarly, sending tapes to the missionary is not encouraged. Missionaries live on a high spiritual plane, and too often the voices of family members bring pains of homesickness and set back the adjustment process. One mission president told me that the only missionary he lost in three years was a young man who was homesick but was just settling down when he received a tape from his family; he left his mission the next day. Also, be concerned if the missionary calls home without the mission president's approval.

Don't plan to visit your missionary in the field. This could be time-consuming and could adversely affect the spirit of the missionary and slow the work.

Do encourage the missionary to come home without undue delay when his mission is completed. Lengthy trips after the mission are discouraged because in such a situation the spirit of the mission begins to dwindle and the missionary comes home more as a tourist than as a returned missionary. A few days to see cultural or Church historic sites on the way home should be sufficient. Let all the people of the ward who have prayed for him and encouraged him see the returned missionary with the spirit of his mission radiating from his countenance. The sooner he gets home, the more spiritual he will be. If the parents plan on picking up their missionary, they should not plan an extended trip before returning home.

Do contact the Missionary Department if there has been a natural disaster or other such tragedy in the area where the missionary is serving. The Missionary Department maintains regular contact with all missionary areas of the world, however, and if there is a tragedy affecting the missionaries, they will contact the parents through local priesthood leaders.

Parents should prepare their youth for missionary service from a very early age. The projected missions might be mentioned in prayers and also be the subject of family home evening from time to time. They may well be a regular topic of conversation in the home. The parents can also make arrangements to have one of the missionary discussions presented in the home and to familiarize family members with the concepts associated with all the discussions. And the family can friendship at least one nonmember family, as the President of the Church asks each family to do, as part of the program and to develop referrals for the missionaries.

The good example of parents cannot be overemphasized. One missionary who was about to complete his mission said: "I have to bear my testimony in two parts. First, my testimony before I came on my mission. I knew the gospel was true because Dad said it was true, and Dad is a good man, and I knew I could trust him. Dad wanted me to go on a mission and I felt good about going.

"My testimony now is that I have read and pondered and prayed about the Book of Mormon and I know it is true. Because the Book of Mormon is true, I know that Joseph Smith was a prophet of God. Because the Book of Mormon is true, I know that Jesus Christ is the Son of God and that this is the true church."

This missionary's testimony had its beginning because he trusted his father enough to go into the mission field. From there he gained his own testimony of the truthfulness of the work.

If a prospective missionary has no father, or if the parents are not members of the Church, the responsibility for missionary preparation rests with the local priesthood leaders and the prospective missionary himself. Home teachers, quorum leaders, and the bishop must see to it that as many as possible of these experiences we have discussed are provided the young man as he prepares for a mission. The personal example of local priesthood leaders is also vital. For instance, a bishop or quorum leader will have a difficult time persuading a prospective missionary to get a haircut and dress conservatively if he does not set such an example himself.

Every parent, priesthood leader, and leader of youth in the Church has the responsibility of setting a good example and encouraging the youth of the Church to prepare themselves for missionary service. May the Lord help each of us and make us equal to the task.

Index

—A—

Addiction, 10
Adjustment, challenge of (story),
    20-21
  normal, 6-7
  period of, 25
Alma, on testimony, 33
Alternatives, 12
Ammon, on service, 29
Article of Faith, fifth, 1, 5
Assignments, mission, 2-3

—B—

Baptism, 42
Benjamin, King, on indebtedness
    to the Lord, 16-17
  on service, 29
Bible, 43
Bishop, responsibility of, 73
Blessings, 51-52
  patriarchal, 9-10
Book of Mormon, 39-43, 70
  message of, 41-42
  purpose of, 41
  (quotation), 43
  value in reading, 54-55
Branches, 46

—C—

Call, mission, acceptance of, 3
  divine nature of, 57-61
  receiving a, 1-5
Calls, telephone, 71
Capability, 6-10
Cars (story), 17
Change, 63-64
Church court, 14, 65
Church Missionary Fund, 15
Church of Jesus Christ of
    Latter-day Saints, The, 42,
    43
  President of, 3
Commitment, 34
  (story), 34-35, 36-37
Companion, 45
  adjusting to a, 27-31
  junior, 30-31, 45
  senior, 30, 45
Companionship, missionary,
    27-28

successful, traits of, 28-30
  (story), 29
Council of the Twelve, 2
Conditioning, 11
Confession, 13, 14
Consistency, importance of, 22-23
Conversion, 38
Cowdery, Oliver, 41

—D—

Decision, 18-19
  (story), 18-19
Decisions, advance, 10-11
  (story), 25
Desire, 17-19
Determination (story), 12
Differences, acceptance of, 29
Difficulties, conquering of (story),
  21-22
  overcoming of, 28
Discipline, 69
Discomforts, 62
Discussions, 48
  missionary, 38
Districts, 45, 46
Doubts, 7
  proper handling of, 36

—E—

Embarrassment, freedom from,
  11
Endurance (quotation), 56
Evans, Richard L., on life, 11
Examination, physical, 2
Expectations, 20-23
Experience, mission, uniqueness
  of, 7
Experiences, missionary, 22
  spiritual, 33

—F—

Faith, 33-34
  (quotation), 34
Families, teaching and
  conversion of, 66-67

Family, golden, 49
  nonmember, friendshipping of,
  73
Father, role of, 67-68
Fear, 6
Finances, 14-17
Forgiveness, 28
Form, acceptance, 3
  medical, 2, 62
  missionary recommendation, 2
Friendships, 27

—G—

Girl friend, 63-65
Goals (quotation), 11
Gospel, effect of, in people's lives,
  50-51
Grant, Heber J. (story), 36-37
Grooming, 70

—H—

Habits, personal, 10, 69
  (quotation), 10
Handbook, missionary, 37
Handicaps, missionary service
  prevented by, 9
Happiness, 70
Harris, Martin, 41
Health, physical and emotional, 2
Home, lessons learned at, 68-70
  practice of gospel principles at,
  66-70
Home evenings, 67
Home teachers, 73
Honesty, 61
  importance of, in confidential
  interviews, 14

—I—

Immorality, 10, 14
Interview, bishop's, 1-2
  mission president's, 45
  stake president's, 2, 4
Investigators, change in lives of,
  38

Involvements, romantic, 65

—J—

Jesus Christ, 41, 43
    appearance of, to Nephites, 40
"Jet lag," 24

—L—

Lamoni, King, 29
Language Training Mission, 3, 8
    four objectives of, 4-5
Leaders, district, 45
    priesthood, 74
    quorum, 73
    zone, 45
Leadership, 70
Learning, 8
Letter, containing mission call, 3
    "Dear John," 63
    from mission president, 3
Letters, 48-56, 71

—M—

Manners, 69
Meetings, zone motivational and
    development, 45
Memorizing, 8
Mission, adjustment to a, 24-26
    call to serve a, 1-5
    completion of, 57-62, 72
"Mission, getting the spirit of
    your," 8
Missionaries, full-time, 46-47
    returned, 21
Missionary, 45
    age of, 1
    calling of, 1-5
    doubts of, 35
    financial support of, 15
    letters from a, 48-56
    new, 30
    newly called, feelings of, 7
    prospective, doubts of, 7
    questions for prospective, 6-19
    romantic feelings of, 65

waiting for a, 63-65
Missionary Department, 2, 3, 72
Missionary Executive
    Committee, 14
Missionary Home, 3, 4, 8
    office staff, 45
Mission field, 8
Mission president, 4, 44, 45
    assistants to, 44-45
    counselors to, 44
    missionary letters to, 45
Missions, organization of, 44-46
    preparations of youth for, 72
Mistake (quotation), 10
Moroni, 40
    on gaining a testimony, 38
Mormon, 40
Mother, role of, 68

—N—

Nephi, on obedience, 31
Nourishment (quotation), 33
Now, importance of, 11, 12

—O—

Obedience (quotation), 31, 69
Organization, district and stake,
    46-47
    mission, 44-46

—P—

Parents, do's and don'ts for, 71-73
    good example of, 73
Parker, Captain John, 12
Paul, the apostle, on how to serve,
    26
Prayer, 68
Preparation, honest, 61
    missionary, 73
Principles, gospel, orderly
    sequence of, 38
    practiced at home, 66
Problems, emotional, 9
    health, 9

physical and emotional, 62
Profanity, 10
Program, missionary, emphasis
    of, 66
Prophets, Book of Mormon, 39

—R—

Repentance, 12, 13, 42
Relationship, between sacrifice
    and success, 15
    working, 28
Resolution, to complete mission, 9
Respect, 68
Revolution, American, first battle
    of (story), 12
Rules, missionary, 30, 37

—S—

Sacrifice, 15
    financial, in support of
        missionaries (story), 16
Salvation, plan of, 42
Savings account, mission, 15
Scriptures, 69-70
    daily reading of, 70
    value of (quotation), 70
Servant, becoming a, 29
Service, opportunities for, 10
    (quotation), 29
    successful missionary, 61-62
Sin (quotation), 12
Smith, Joseph, 40, 42
    on Book of Mormon, 42
    on polishing process, 21
Stand, taking a, 13-14
Stevenson, Robert Louis, on
    weaknesses, 61
Success, 15, 70
Support, financial, responsibility
    for, 15

—T—

Tape recordings, 65, 71
Taylor, John, 36-37
Temptation, 18-19
Testimony, 32-38, 49
    confirmation of, 37-38
    (quotation), 34, 36
    (story), 73
Transgressions, previous,
    clearing up of, 13-14
Trials (story), 21-22
Trips, following completion of
    mission, 72
Truth, 10, 36
Type, learning to (story), 7

—U—

Uniform System for Teaching
    Families, 48

—W—

Wards, 46
Weaknesses (quotation), 61
Whitmer, David, 41
Witnesses, testimony of the
    Three, 41
Work, 69
    ability to, 29
    hard, 30
    missionary, 24-25, 49
Worthiness, 10-14

—Y—

"Years, the best two," 21

—Z—

Zones, 45